NEW MEXICO

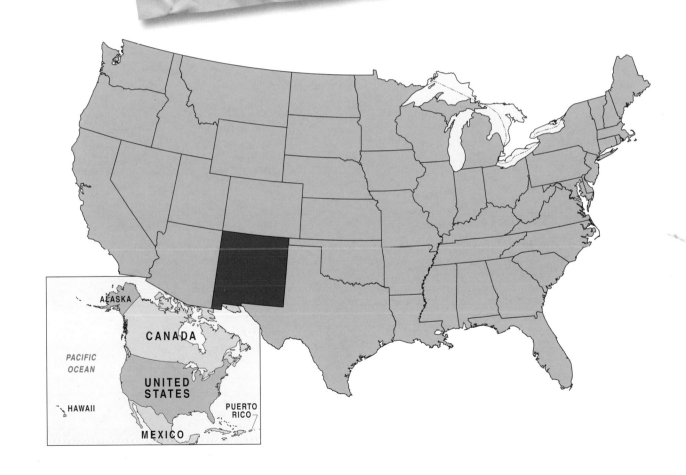

NEW MEXICO

HELLO U.S.A.

by Theresa S. Early

Lerner Publications Company

You'll find this picture of a Navajo rug at the beginning of each chapter. The rug was made by Navajo weavers during the late 1800s. This era of Navajo art is known as the Transitional Period. At this time, the Navajo began trading with European settlers, allowing weavers to use materials such as manufactured cloth and dyes. Navajo New Mexicans continue to make beautiful, high-quality rugs.

Cover (left): Taos Pueblo. Cover (right): Claret cup cactus in Valley of Fires State Park. Pages 2–3: White Sands National Monument. Page 3: The state capitol building in Santa Fe.

This book is available in two editions:
Library binding by Lerner Publications Company, a division of Lerner Publishing Group
Soft cover by First Avenue Editions, an imprint of Lerner Publishing Group
241 First Avenue North
Minneapolis, MN 55401 U.S.A.

Website address: www.lernerbooks.com

Library of Congress Cataloging-in-Publication Data

Early, Theresa S., 1957–
    New Mexico / by Theresa S. Early (Rev. and expanded 2nd ed.)
        p.   cm. — (Hello U.S.A.)
    Summary: Presents the geography, history, people, economy, and environment of New Mexico.
    Includes bibliographical references and index.
    ISBN: 0–8225–4096–7 (lib. bdg. : alk paper)
    ISBN: 0–8225–0789–7 (pbk. : alk paper)
    1. New Mexico—Juvenile literature. [1. New Mexico.] I. Title. II. Series.
F796.3.E18 2003
978.9—dc21   2001008654

Manufactured in the United States of America
1 2 3 4 5 6 – JR – 08 07 06 05 04 03

CONTENTS

THE LAND: Mountains, Mesas, and Miles of Sand 7

THE HISTORY: Settlers and Scientists 17

PEOPLE & ECONOMY: Cultural and Natural Resources 40

THE ENVIRONMENT: Watching Over Nuclear Waste 51

ALL ABOUT NEW MEXICO 60

Fun Facts 60
State Song 62
A New Mexico Recipe 63
Historical Timeline 64
Outstanding New Mexicans .66
Facts-at-a-Glance 70
Places to Visit 74
Annual Events 76
Learn More about New Mexico 77
Pronunciation Guide 80
Glossary 81
Index 82

THE LAND

Mountains, Mesas, and Miles of Sand

f the 50 states, New Mexico is the fifth largest in area. It offers miles and miles of unending beauty, from forested mountains to colorful deserts and vast plains. Because of its breathtaking scenery, New Mexico is often called the Land of Enchantment.

New Mexico lies in the heart of the Southwest. The state is bordered on the west by Arizona, to the northwest by Utah, on the north by Colorado, and on the east by Texas and Oklahoma. Texas and the country of Mexico mark New Mexico's southern border.

Opposite page: In northwestern New Mexico, the Bisti Badlands Wilderness Area features a striking landscape of dramatic rock formations.

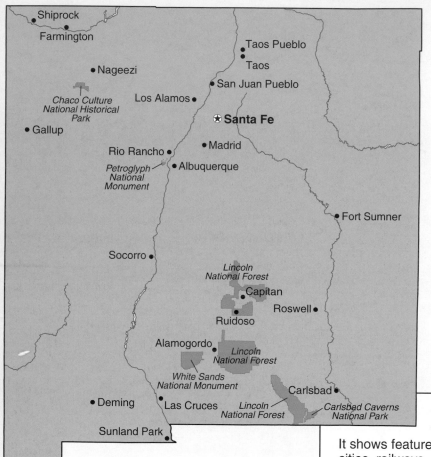

- Shiprock
- Farmington
- Nageezi
- Taos Pueblo
- Taos
- San Juan Pueblo
- Los Alamos
Chaco Culture
National Historical
Park
- ⊛ **Santa Fe**
- Gallup
- Rio Rancho
- Madrid
Petroglyph
National
Monument
- Albuquerque
- Fort Sumner
- Socorro
Lincoln
National Forest
- Capitan
- Roswell
- Ruidoso
- Alamogordo
Lincoln
National Forest
White Sands
National Monument
- Carlsbad
- Deming
- Las Cruces
Lincoln
National Forest
Carlsbad Caverns
National Park
- Sunland Park

NEW MEXICO
Political Map

⊛   State capital

0	30	60 Miles

0	30	60	90	120 Kilometers

The drawing of New Mexico on this page is called a political map. It shows features created by people, including cities, railways, and parks. The map on the facing page is called a physical map. It shows physical features of New Mexico, such as mountains, rivers, and lakes. The colors represent a range of elevations, or heights above sea level (see legend box). This map also shows the geographical regions of New Mexico.

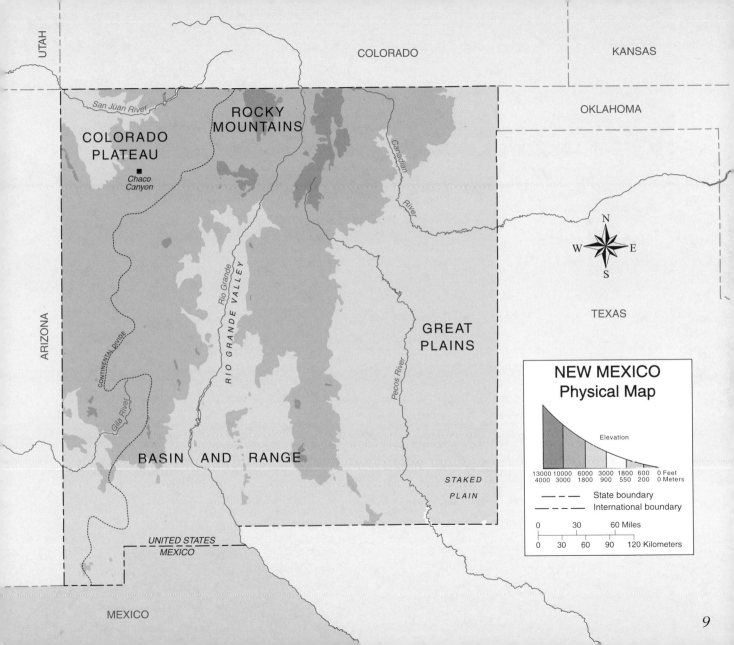

UTAH

COLORADO

KANSAS

OKLAHOMA

San Juan River

ROCKY
MOUNTAINS

COLORADO
PLATEAU

*Chaco
Canyon*

Canadian

River

ARIZONA

CONTINENTAL DIVIDE

Gila River

RIO GRANDE

RIO GRANDE VALLEY

TEXAS

N
W   E
S

GREAT
PLAINS

Pecos River

BASIN   AND   RANGE

*STAKED
PLAIN*

UNITED STATES
MEXICO

NEW MEXICO
Physical Map

Elevation

| 13000 | 10000 | 6000 | 3000 | 1800 | 600 | 0 Feet |
| 4000 | 3000 | 1800 | 900 | 550 | 200 | 0 Meters |

– – –   State boundary
– – –   International boundary

| 0 | 30 | 60 Miles |

| 0 | 30 | 60 | 90 | 120 Kilometers |

MEXICO

9

The sharp peaks of the Rocky Mountains dominate the landscape of north central New Mexico.

New Mexico is divided into four regions—the Rocky Mountains, the Colorado Plateau, the Basin and Range, and the Great Plains. The first three regions have mountains, but all of the state is higher—and much of it is drier—than most other places in the United States.

The Rocky Mountain region in north central New Mexico is named after the chain of mountains that stretches across it. Reaching from Alaska to New Mexico, the Rocky Mountains (also called the Rockies) form the longest mountain system in North America.

The Rockies were formed millions of years ago by volcanoes that spewed layers of hot liquid rock called **lava.** The lava cooled and hardened into mountains. Wind and water gradually wore them down to their present shape.

The Rockies also form much of North America's Continental Divide—a ridge of high land separating the rivers that flow east from those that flow west. In New Mexico, the divide runs through a short stretch of the Rocky Mountains, through the Colorado Plateau and the Basin and Range.

The Colorado Plateau in northwestern New Mexico is a rocky region made up of mountains and **plateaus,** or flat highlands. Rivers have cut deep canyons and strange, beautiful rock sculptures into the plateau. Isolated flat-topped hills, called **mesas,** dot the land.

Enchanted Mesa in west central New Mexico rises more than 400 feet above the surrounding land.

The Basin and Range region covers much of southern and central New Mexico. Some of the mountain ranges in the region rise more than 10,000 feet. In between the ranges lie broad valleys, or **basins,** that are so dry they are considered **deserts.** Most of New Mexico's people live in or near the Basin and Range in the Rio Grande Valley. Farms in the valley yield crops such as chili peppers, cotton, and pecans.

The bright flowers of the cholla cactus *(inset)* bloom in New Mexico's Basin and Range region. Sand as white as snow glitters at White Sands National Monument *(right),* a desert that lies in south central New Mexico.

Miles of rich grazing land stretch across southeastern New Mexico's Staked Plain.

The Great Plains region covers the eastern third of the state. The region is wide and nearly flat, although it has deep valleys and mesas in the north. Most of the state's cattle are raised on the Great Plains.

Few rivers flow year round in New Mexico. Heat and lack of rain cause many of them to dry up during the summer. The state's longest and most important river is the Rio Grande, which flows south through the entire state.

The wide waters of the Rio Grande ("big river" in Spanish) flow south through New Mexico.

Other chief rivers include the Pecos, the Canadian, the Gila, and the San Juan. The Pecos and Canadian Rivers, as well as the Rio Grande, flow on the east side of the Continental Divide. The Gila and San Juan Rivers flow on the west side.

New Mexico's elevation, or height above sea level, ranges from about 3,000 to 13,000 feet. Areas at high elevations are colder than areas at low elevations, so the state's climate varies greatly.

In the low southwestern deserts, summer temperatures can be more than 100° F, and winter temperatures hover around 40° F. Snow falls almost everywhere in New Mexico, but the low, dry areas of the state receive only about 2 inches per year. Rainfall is scarce throughout most of the state. Dry conditions put parts of New Mexico in danger of wildfires. In May 2000, a fire near Los Alamos destroyed thousands of acres of land.

In the northern mountains, summer temperatures are cooler than in the south, averaging just below 70° F. Winter temperatures in the north can be bitterly cold but average about 24° F. On the slopes above the northern resort town of Taos, skiers expect a lot of powdery snow—more than 300 inches a year.

New Mexico's rivers and streams are filled with bass, catfish, trout, and other catches for young fishers.

Because the weather conditions vary throughout New Mexico, the state contains a wide range of plants and animals. Cacti and shrubs, such as prickly pear, cholla, and mesquite, thrive in the desert. Horned toads, rattlesnakes, and poisonous spiders—including the tarantula and the black widow—also do well in the desert heat.

In the mountains, piñon trees and alpine fungi grow. Marmots and pikas, two kinds of small furry mammals, live at the state's highest elevations. Bighorn sheep and elk climb a bit lower. On the Great Plains and lower mountains, pronghorn antelope and mule deer roam.

The prickly pear cactus *(above left)* blooms in New Mexico's deserts. The New Mexican Rockies are home to the sure-footed bighorn sheep *(left)*.

THE HISTORY

Settlers and Scientists

he first people known to live in North America were hunters who probably left Asia at least 12,000 years ago. Eventually, these ancestors of modern-day Native Americans spread throughout North and South America.

Among the first peoples to build permanent villages and farms in the Southwest were the Mogollon and the Anasazi. *Anasazi* is a Navajo Indian word meaning "ancient ones." The early Anasazi are also called the Basket Makers because they were so skillful at weaving baskets. The Anasazi grew corn and beans and trained dogs for hunting. The Indians also made pottery.

Hundreds of years ago, the Anasazi Indians of Chaco Canyon lived in huge complexes such as the Pueblo Bonito. Modern-day visitors can see the ruins of these enormous structures.

Using stone or sun-dried mud, the Anasazi built villages in the region that later became northwestern New Mexico. Each village was made up of one large building that was several stories high, like an apartment house. The Anasazi left their villages in the late 1200s after a long **drought,** or dry spell, made farming impossible. They moved to other parts of what became New Mexico.

Nomadic, or traveling, tribes of Navajo and of Apache Indians eventually moved to the Southwest. The Navajo lived in small family groups. Their homes, called hogans, were built from logs and earth. The Apache traveled in large groups. They lived in tepees made of animal hides or in grass dwellings called wickiups.

Navajo Indians call Shiprock, a large landform in northwestern New Mexico, the "rock with wings" and honor it as a sacred site.

By the early 1500s, American Indians lived throughout what later became New Mexico. At the same time, Spain was conquering Indian villages to the south, in what later became the country of Mexico. The Spaniards took a fortune in gold and jewels from the Indians. Eager to find more wealth, the king of Spain set up a Spanish **colony,** or settlement, in Mexico.

Hoping to find the Seven Cities of Cibola, Coronado led his troops to the region that later became New Mexico.

Francisco Vásquez de Coronado, a Spanish governor in Mexico, led the first major European expedition to the New Mexico area. In 1540 the

group began a long journey in search of more gold. Coronado was looking for the Seven Cities of Cibola—seven cities rich in gold that were rumored to lie north of Mexico.

Instead of gold, Coronado found descendants of the Anasazi living in multistoried villages. The explorers were impressed by the design of the villages, which they called *pueblos* (the Spanish word for "towns"). The Spaniards also named the people who lived in these villages Pueblos.

Pueblo Indians have been living in Taos Pueblo since the 1200s, making it the only building in the United States to be continuously inhabited for so long. Spanish explorers first reached the pueblo in the 1500s.

Spanish settlers preached Catholicism to the native peoples of New Mexico.

By 1542 Coronado and his expedition had returned to Mexico to report their failure. Although no gold had been found, rumors still flew that the area just north of Mexico was full of riches—it was a "new" Mexico. New Mexico is what the area has been called ever since.

In 1610 Pedro de Peralta, a Spanish official, established the first permanent Spanish settlement in New Mexico. This settlement, Santa Fe, served as the capital of the colony of New Mexico.

Since earlier attempts to find gold in New Mexico had been fruitless, the goal of the colonists changed. They decided to spread the official religion of Spain—Catholicism. To turn the Pueblo Indians into Catholics, the Spaniards outlawed Indian religions.

In addition, the Spaniards collected food from the Indians as a tax and forced them to farm land that the Spaniards had taken. To make matters worse, smallpox, measles, and other European diseases swept through the villages. One out of every ten Pueblo Indians died of smallpox in 1640.

The Pueblo Revolt of 1680

During the 1600s, the Spaniards tried to make the Pueblo Indians dress like Europeans and speak Spanish. They also tried to stamp out the Pueblo religions, replacing them with a very different faith—Catholicism. Catholics worshiped one god, while the Pueblos worshiped several spirits. Some Pueblos accepted the Catholic religion, or parts of it. A Pueblo Indian artist, for example, painted the Madonna *(right)* with Pueblo Indian features. But others rejected Catholicism entirely.

Popé, an Indian religious leader from San Juan Pueblo, encouraged Indians to remain true to their religion. In 1675 Spanish soldiers arrested 47 Pueblo religious leaders—including Popé. The Spaniards hanged three of the men and whipped and jailed most of the others. After Popé was released from jail, he helped plan a rebellion.

On August 10, 1680, Pueblo Indians throughout the colony of New Mexico attacked Spanish villages, killing more than 400 Spaniards and running the rest

out of New Mexico. The Pueblo Revolt of 1680 marked Spain's first loss of an entire colony. Spain reconquered New Mexico in 1693, prompting many Pueblos to leave the area. But those who stayed refused to live under the old Spanish rules. Pueblo religions and culture are still alive in modern-day New Mexico.

The peaceful villages of Pueblo Indians were raided by nomadic tribes for goods such as clay pots.

The nomadic Apache and Navajo were more difficult for the Spaniards to conquer. On horses stolen from the Spaniards, the nomads raided both Spanish and Pueblo villages to get items they did not make or raise themselves. They stole food, animals, and blankets.

Overall, the colony of New Mexico was poor. Supplies were sent from Mexico City (the capital of Mexico) only once or twice a year. This was partly because travelers had to cross the Jornada del Muerto, or Journey of Death—90 miles of trail with no water. Yet New Mexicans were not allowed to buy or sell goods from anywhere else. They raised or made almost everything they needed. But some items, such as iron pots and sugar, were very scarce.

In the early 1700s, Comanche Indians moved into New Mexico from the northwest. Their raids on the Spaniards and the Pueblos were fierce. Sometimes the Comanche were joined by Ute Indians from the north. By the 1740s, the Comanche had taken control of much of eastern New Mexico.

The excellent horseback-riding skills of the Comanche Indians helped them to raid New Mexican settlements in the 1700s.

About 30 years later, the Spaniards and the Pueblo Indians joined forces in a successful battle against the Comanche. By 1786 the New Mexican and the Comanche leaders had signed a peace **treaty,** an agreement to end the warfare.

In 1821 Mexico gained independence from Spain. For the first time, New Mexicans were governed by Mexican leaders, not by the king of Spain. New Mexicans celebrated because Mexico granted them new freedoms, including the right to trade with outsiders.

William Becknell, a trader from Missouri, heard of Mexico's independence and headed for New Mexico. He was the first trader from the United States to reach Santa Fe. Becknell found New Mexicans eager for the goods he offered and willing to pay high prices for them.

Trade between the United States and New Mexico flourished. Traders drove covered wagons along a well-marked route called the Santa Fe Trail, which ran from Independence, Missouri, to Santa Fe. Santa Fe began to grow. New settlers came to town

selling hats, gloves, silverware, books, spices, medicine, and paint to eager customers. **Anglos,** as these settlers from the United States were called, also built stores and banks.

Traders and settlers on the Santa Fe Trail streamed into New Mexico during the 1800s.

As more U.S. citizens moved southwestward, the U.S. government became interested in New Mexico and other Mexican territories. When Mexico refused to sell its territories to the United States, the two countries began fighting what became known as the Mexican War (1846–1848).

In 1846 U.S. troops arrived in Santa Fe prepared for battle. But the New Mexican governor, fearing defeat, had already dismissed his troops and fled south. In other Mexican territories, battles continued until 1848, when the war officially ended. As a result of its victory, the United States gained control of most of the Southwest, including New Mexico.

In 1846 General Stephen Kearny claimed New Mexico for the United States. New Mexico didn't officially become a U.S. territory until after the Mexican War ended in 1848.

In 1850 the U.S. government established boundaries for the Territory of New Mexico. It included modern-day New Mexico and Arizona and parts of Colorado and Nevada. In 1853 the United States paid Mexico for more land at the southern edge of the territory. This deal was known as the Gadsden Purchase.

As a U.S. territory, New Mexico began to change. The U.S. government offered free farmland to new settlers, attracting many Anglos to the area. Others came to make money in trade. The Spaniards and the Pueblo Indians lost much of their land to Anglo settlers.

Some of the Anglos came from Southern states, where slavery was allowed. In 1861 the Civil War broke out between the Southern states and the Northern states, which wanted to end slavery. The Territory of New Mexico officially sided with the North, or the Union. But a lot of U.S. army officers in New Mexico sided with the South, or the Confederacy. Many of these officers resigned from the U.S. Army so that they could join Confederate forces.

The Confederates quickly captured much of New Mexico, including Santa Fe and the growing city of Albuquerque. The Union army recaptured New Mexico after defeating the Confederates at the Battle of Glorieta Pass in 1862. The Union victory kept the Confederates from controlling the Southwest and California.

During the Civil War, the Union fought the Confederacy for New Mexico and other southwestern territories at the Battle of Glorieta Pass.

While army troops were busy fighting the Civil War, the Apache and Navajo increased their raiding. But by 1863, U.S. troops had defeated the Indians and sent them to a **reservation**—an area of land for Indians to live on. Life on Bosque Redondo Reservation in eastern New Mexico was extremely difficult. The land was too poor and dry to farm, and the Indians could not raise enough food for themselves. Thousands died.

After New Mexican Navajo and Apache Indians were defeated by U.S. soldiers, they were forced to move to the Bosque Redondo Reservation. The journey, which became known to the Navajo as the Long Walk, was long and difficult, and many Indians died.

On their new reservation in northern New Mexico, the Apache worked hard to farm the land and raise healthy crops.

Eventually, the Apache simply left the reservation. Some went back to their homeland in south central New Mexico. The U.S. government allowed them to stay and simply created another reservation there. Other Apache were settled on a reservation in northern New Mexico. The Navajo were also allowed to return to their own lands.

Meanwhile traders and ranchers were busy in New Mexico. The territory's grasslands were excellent for grazing sheep, which had become a big money-maker for New Mexico's farmers. After the Civil War, corn, wheat, and cattle gained in importance. Soon, trails crisscrossed the state as ranchers drove cattle from their grazing ranges to the nearest market.

Silver and gold mining had become important in southwestern New Mexico by the 1870s. Towns grew up overnight where ore was found. But as soon as the ore was gone, the miners moved away, leaving only ghost towns.

In the mid and late 1800s, miners looking to strike it rich flocked to western states like New Mexico.

In 1878 train tracks were laid across New Mexico. These tracks made it possible to carry cattle, sheep, and metal ore to market on trains. Albuquerque became the railroad and business center of New Mexico.

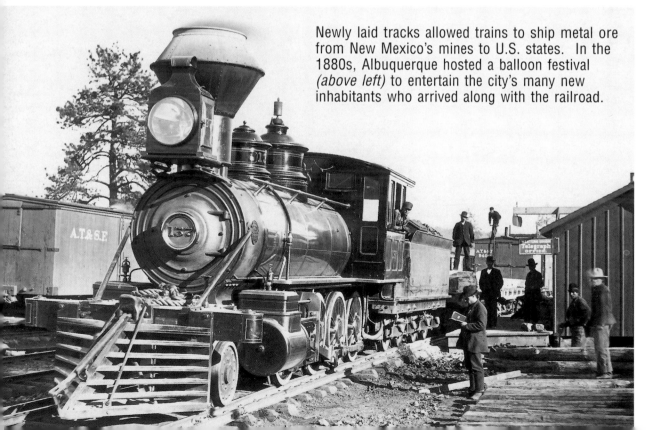

Newly laid tracks allowed trains to ship metal ore from New Mexico's mines to U.S. states. In the 1880s, Albuquerque hosted a balloon festival *(above left)* to entertain the city's many new inhabitants who arrived along with the railroad.

Legends from a Lawless Land

When people think of the Wild West, they often picture scenes from old western movies. New Mexico of the late 1800s was more than the harmless loud saloons and

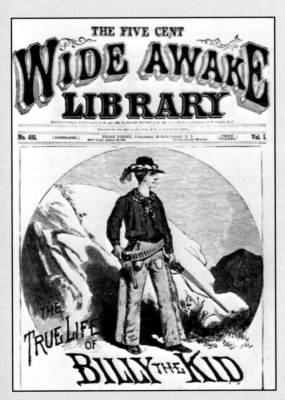

gambling halls on the silver screen—it was the real Wild West. Few laws—and even fewer law enforcers—existed in the territory. Feuds broke out over almost anything, and the result was sometimes deadly.

Some feuds turned into wars. During the 1870s, for example, ranchers in Lincoln County, New Mexico, fought over land and over who would supply cattle to the U.S. Army, which paid high prices for beef. During what became known as the Lincoln County War, ranchers hired gunmen to threaten or kill competing ranchers. Cattle baron John Tunstall hired a young gunslinger named William H. Bonney, better known as Billy the Kid.

When Tunstall was shot to death in 1878 by an enemy, Billy the Kid declared he would kill anyone involved in the shooting. Bloody feuds followed, and U.S. Army troops were brought in to restore order. But the Lincoln County War did not officially end until Sheriff Pat Garret shot and killed Billy the Kid near Fort Sumner, New Mexico, in 1881.

In the early 1900s, New Mexico still seemed like a foreign place to many Americans. Most New Mexicans spoke Spanish. Nevertheless, on January 6, 1912, New Mexico became the 47th state.

During the Great Depression, the long economic slump of the 1930s, jobs were hard to find. To make matters worse, drought ravaged the state. Some areas were so dry from lack of rain that the wind whipped up the loose soil and blew black clouds of dust across the land. Crops failed and animals died. These areas were part of the **Dust Bowl,** the

During the days of the Dust Bowl, huge clouds of sand filled the air.

Sunday April 14 1935

name given to a section of the United States that suffered from severe droughts.

The outbreak of World War II in 1939 brought improved economic times to New Mexico. In 1942 J. Robert Oppenheimer, a scientist, chose Los Alamos Ranch School outside Santa Fe as the site to do research on a secret military project.

Posters printed in English, Spanish, and several Indian languages urged New Mexicans to support the government during World War II.

NEW MEXICO

BUY   BUY

COMPRE
COMPRE
COMPRE
COMPRE

AWONG-GEEH
ACOO-MAN
DA-AH

WAR

BONDS AND STAMPS

At Los Alamos, scientists developed the world's first atomic bomb, a highly destructive nuclear weapon. It was first tested near Alamogordo, New Mexico, on July 16, 1945. People throughout the state noticed the flash and blast of the bomb, but few knew what had really happened. Some said the sun came up twice that day.

The following month, the United States dropped two atomic bombs on Japan, bringing World War II to an end. In the decades following the war, government projects at various laboratories in New Mexico continued to employ many New Mexicans. Many of the researchers at these labs studied nuclear weapons that were similar to the atomic bomb.

During the late 1980s and the 1990s, research on making and testing weapons decreased. But

Located in Socorro, New Mexico, the Very Large Array (VLA) radio telescope began operating in 1981.

employees at scientific labs in New Mexico continue to work on important projects, from developing new medical techniques to researching the use of nuclear energy. Some of these labs are owned by the government. Other labs, such as the Sandia National Laboratories in Albuquerque, are owned by private businesses. Other high-tech ventures in the state include the Very Large Array (VLA) radio telescope in Socorro. The VLA, which had its twentieth anniversary in 2001, collects information about outer space by taking detailed photographs of the stars and planets.

Along with modern scientific research, New Mexicans still practice age-old traditions. Spanish is spoken every day by many residents. Native American ceremonies take place regularly, and pottery is made the way it was hundreds of years ago. New Mexico's history and cultures still flavor daily life.

PEOPLE & ECONOMY

Cultural and Natural Resources

New Mexico seems very different from other states in the country. The mix of Pueblo, Navajo, Apache, **Latino,** and Anglo cultures gives the state a flavor all its own.

The variety of people, art, scenery, and jobs has attracted many newcomers to New Mexico. Many of the new residents flock to the state's three largest cities—Albuquerque, Las Cruces, and Santa Fe (the capital). The population of Rio Rancho, the state's fourth-largest city, grew almost 60 percent between 1990 and 2000.

Using a traditional loom, this Navajo woman weaves a wool rug. Famous for their detailed designs, Navajo rugs are a popular product of New Mexico.

Just over half of the 1.8 million New Mexicans claim Latin American or Native American ancestry, or both. One out of every 10 people is Native American—a larger percentage than in most other states. The state's many reservations and pueblos are home to Navajo, Apache, Ute, and Pueblo peoples.

Albuquerque was settled by Spaniards in 1706, and some of the original Spanish buildings are still standing, such as the San Felipe de Neri Church in the Old Town section of the city. Almost 450,000 modern-day New Mexicans call Albuquerque home.

Shoppers admire art, jewelry, and other goods at Santa Fe's Indian Market *(below)*. Indian fry bread *(below bottom)* makes a tasty snack for hungry visitors.

Most of the state's reservations are poor, but several earn money from their mineral-rich land. The Navajo allow oil wells and mines on their reservation. Some lumber companies pay the Apache for the right to cut down trees on reservation land. In addition, the Apache have built tourist resorts that offer hunting, fishing, golfing, and skiing.

Anglos—people without Latin American or American Indian heritage—make up almost half of New Mexico's population. African Americans and Asian Americans together make up less than 3 percent of the state's population.

Each cultural group in New Mexico proudly displays its traditional artwork. Every day, Native Americans line the plaza in front of the Palace of the Governors in Santa Fe to sell jewelry, weavings, paintings, and pottery. The best Native American artwork is sold at the Indian Market, held every summer in Santa Fe.

During the holidays, glowing luminarias—candles placed in sand-filled bags—light the streets of New Mexico's Latino neighborhoods.

The Spanish markets, also held each year in Santa Fe, offer crafts, such as religious wood carvings and hand-painted tiles. And since the 1920s, Taos and Santa Fe have been home to large groups of Anglo artists and writers. The Santa Fe Opera and Santa Fe Community Theater add to the state capital's reputation as a fine arts center.

Among the state's many historical and fine arts museums are the Museum of New Mexico in Santa Fe and the Indian Pueblo Cultural Center in Albuquerque. The National Atomic Museum in Albuquerque and the Bradbury Science Museum in Los Alamos provide a history of nuclear research.

Two young Latinas *(right)* at a festival in Taos proudly display a colorful piñata, a candy-filled decoration. Brightly colored hot-air balloons like the one below float above Albuquerque during the International Balloon Fiesta.

The International Balloon Fiesta, held every October in Albuquerque, has been called the most photographed event in the world. Hundreds of hot-air balloons fill the air at this colorful display. The New Mexico State Fair in Albuquerque includes a rodeo that is the largest in the world. Gallup hosts the Inter-Tribal Indian Ceremonial each year. At this event, native tribes from the United States and Mexico gather for rodeos, dances, parades, and an art show.

Sports lovers can watch horse racing at tracks in Albuquerque, Santa Fe, Ruidoso, and Sunland Park. Crowds cheer on the University of New Mexico's basketball and football teams. And hockey fans head to Albuquerque to see the New Mexico Scorpions, a professional minor-league team in the Central Hockey League.

New Mexico offers athletes and nature lovers a wide variety of activities. Hiking, horseback riding, fishing, white-water rafting, and skiing keep New Mexicans and visitors busy outdoors year round.

Brave boaters can test their skill against the quickly flowing waters of the Rio Grande.

The U.S. government employs New Mexicans to take care of the campgrounds and trails of the state's national parks *(left).* Snowy slopes near Santa Fe provide winter fun for residents and tourists *(below).*

New Mexico's outdoor activities and other attractions draw millions of tourists to the state each year. People who serve these tourists and other people have service jobs. Service workers make up 62 percent of New Mexico's workforce. These employees include salesclerks, ski instructors, and restaurant and hotel staff.

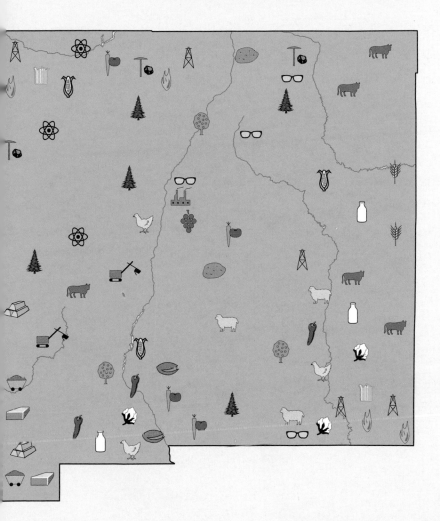

NEW MEXICO
Economic Map

The symbols on this map show where different economic activities take place in New Mexico. The legend below explains what each symbol stands for.

	Beef cattle		Manufacturing
	Chili peppers		Milk
	Coal		Natural gas
	Copper		Oil
	Corn		Pecans
	Cotton		Potatoes
	Forest products		Poultry
	Fruit		Sheep
	Gold		Silver
	Grapes		Tourism
	Hay		Uranium
	Iron ore		Vegetables
	Wheat		

The U.S. government employs 20 percent of working New Mexicans. Some of these people manage the state's national parks, forests, and grazing lands. Others work in schools, post offices, and hospitals. Many New Mexicans have jobs with the government's defense and energy departments, studying nuclear energy and science at labs including Los Alamos National Laboratory and White Sands Missile Range.

New Mexico has programs to prepare people for high-technology jobs. The state's labs and high-tech companies hire these trained workers. Some of the companies make computer parts or electrical equipment. Other manufacturers in the state make food products, appliances, and wood products. Manufacturing employs 6 percent of New Mexico's workers.

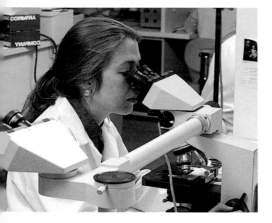

The Kirtland Air Force Base *(top left)* is a military site located in Albuquerque. New Mexico is a leading state in scientific research and technology *(left)*.

Chili peppers don't need much rain and thrive in New Mexico's hot climate.

Mining is another important industry in the state. In fact, New Mexico is a leading mining state, supplying other states in the nation with oil, natural gas, coal, copper, and uranium—a mineral used in creating nuclear energy.

New Mexico's energy resources are being used up as workers mine the state's rich supplies of oil and natural gas. But New Mexico still earns about 80 percent of its mining income from these valuable products. Most of the state's oil and natural gas comes from the southeastern part of the state.

Rainfall is scarce in New Mexico, and much of the state's soil is poor. These two conditions make it impossible for many crops to survive. Only about 4 percent of New Mexico's workers have jobs on farms and ranches.

49

Cattle graze on New Mexico's wide, grassy plains.

Crops that do grow well in the state need to have water channeled to them from streams and rivers. This process, called **irrigation,** allows New Mexicans to harvest chili peppers, pecans, cotton, hay, wheat, corn, and apples. Most of New Mexico's agricultural products come from the Rio Grande Valley and the Great Plains region. Beef cattle, dairy cattle, and sheep graze on ranches throughout the state. In fact, with more than 1.5 million cattle and calves, New Mexico has almost as many cows as people!

Watching Over Nuclear Waste

 ew Mexico's ties to nuclear science go back to the 1940s and to J. Robert Oppenheimer. The state's laboratories are still leaders in nuclear research, and the state has also become a leader in another important and related issue— where to store **nuclear waste.**

Nuclear waste is garbage tainted with **radiation.** The waste may include parts from nuclear bombs, fuel rods from nuclear power plants, or parts from hospital X-ray machines.

During World War II, J. Robert Oppenheimer made New Mexico a center of nuclear research.

Because nuclear waste is **radioactive,** it is dangerous. Radiation gives off invisible rays and particles that can be harmful to humans. Too much radiation can kill living things. It can cause diseases and birth defects. Radiation is especially dangerous because it has no taste or smell. Some kinds of radiation can pass unnoticed through skin, walls, rocks, and metal.

Nuclear waste gives off harmful radiation for a long time—even hundreds of thousands of years. If nuclear waste is so hazardous, why do we continue to produce it?

Tightly sealed buckets hold low-level nuclear waste, including lab coats, rags, rubber gloves, and tools that have been exposed to radioactivity.

Nuclear energy and other sources of radiation have many benefits. Nuclear power plants that produce electricity create much less air pollution than other sources of electricity, such as coal. And X rays help doctors find their patients' ailments. But these benefits leave the country with a problem. Where do we safely store nuclear waste?

Supporters of nuclear power point out that nuclear power plants usually produce very little air pollution.

At one time, Los Alamos dumped nuclear waste in nearby canyons. Some of the waste eventually washed into local streams and rivers. After that, an unusually large number of people who lived downstream from Los Alamos developed cancer.

The U.S. Department of Energy began searching for a spot where nuclear waste could be stored more safely. In the 1970s, government researchers proposed building the Waste Isolation Pilot Plant (WIPP) in New Mexico, near Carlsbad. The plan suggested digging caves thousands of feet under the earth in beds of salt. These caves would then be prepared to hold containers of nuclear waste.

If the plan were approved, WIPP would become the first long-term storage site for low-level nuclear waste from around the country. Low-level nuclear waste includes contaminated gloves and tools used by workers in nuclear power plants and in nuclear weapons laboratories.

In 1979 Congress voted that WIPP should be built. Construction began in the 1980s, but people were still arguing about whether WIPP should be used.

Many New Mexicans approved of WIPP. Some worked at nuclear laboratories or knew someone who did. They knew that people were working to improve the storage systems for nuclear waste.

The Waste Isolation Pilot Plant (WIPP) was built near Carlsbad during the 1980s.

They trusted that the government knew how to handle nuclear waste safely. They also believed that WIPP would employ many people in New Mexico, bringing money to the state. And they realized that the country had already produced tons of low-level nuclear waste and that it was producing more every day. The waste had to be put somewhere.

Other people fought to stop WIPP. They didn't believe that the site would be safe. Over time, nuclear waste changes. It gives off dangerous gases,

WIPP receives low-level nuclear waste from states around the country.

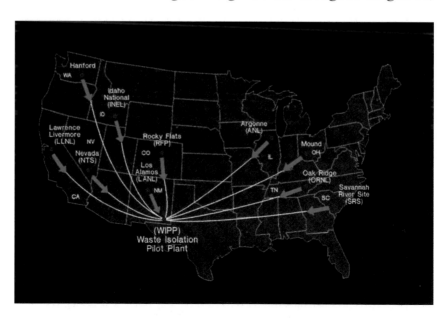

Students test soil for radioactivity with the help of an environmental researcher from WIPP.

and it can become very hot, which might cause the salt in the caves to ooze and crush the containers. Some people feared that the damaged containers would leak radiation, which would then enter New Mexico's underground water supplies. And WIPP would receive tens of thousands of truckloads of waste from around the country. Some of these shipments would travel right through the crowded city of Santa Fe. If a truck carrying nuclear waste were in an accident, the waste could possibly leak, endangering entire communities. Would it be safer to store the waste closer to where it was created?

The government was concerned about safety, too. The Department of Energy asked the U.S. Environmental Protection Agency to study WIPP and see if it could store waste safely. Other programs, including the Transportation Safety Program, researched the best ways to run WIPP.

The first shipment of low-level nuclear waste arrived at WIPP in 1999. Since then, the plant has operated safely. No accidents have occurred. But many New Mexicans are still worried about the long-term dangers of WIPP. Future accidents are another concern. What if someone unknowingly drills into WIPP in 10,000 years? How can the government protect people from the waste for that long?

Even those who support WIPP agree that it's not a total solution. Every day hospitals, nuclear laboratories, and nuclear power plants across the country produce more waste. WIPP only has room for the low-level waste we've already produced. It will take more than 30 years to carry all that waste to WIPP. Many citizens remain concerned about what we will do with the waste we produce in the next 30 years.

New Mexican elementary school students express their worries about nuclear power in a letter to the government.

Fun Facts

In 1950 firefighters rescued a black bear cub from a fire in New Mexico's Lincoln National Forest. They called the cub Smokey Bear, and he became the symbol of the U.S. Forest Service's efforts to prevent forest fires.

Santa Fe, New Mexico, is the oldest capital city in the United States. It was founded in 1610.

At its northwestern corner, New Mexico touches the corners of Arizona, Utah, and Colorado. This point is the only place in the United States where four states meet.

In his new home at the National Zoological Park in Washington, D.C., Smokey Bear visits with a young friend.

In addition to English, most New Mexicans speak at least one other language. Spanish is the second most common language, followed by American Indian tongues, including Apache, Navajo, and several different Pueblo languages.

The world's first atomic bomb was tested in New Mexico at Trinity Site, near Alamogordo, on July 16, 1945.

Every year, residents of Las Cruces, New Mexico, celebrate the Whole Enchilada Fiesta. People attending this three-day event can sample the world's largest enchilada, which is cooked and eaten each year.

Elephant Butte Reservoir is the largest lake in New Mexico. It is 40 miles long and has nearly 200 miles of shoreline. The lake is located near the town of Truth or Consequences.

STATE SONG

New Mexico has two official state songs. "O, Fair New Mexico" was adopted in 1917. It was written by Elizabeth Garrett, whose father was the sherriff who killed outlaw Billy the Kid in 1881. In 1971 New Mexicans adopted "Asi es Nuevo Méjico," which was written in Spanish, as their second official song.

O, FAIR NEW MEXICO

Words and music by Elizabeth Garrett

You can hear "O, Fair New Mexico" by visiting this website:
<http://www.50states.com/songs/newmex.htm>

A NEW MEXICO RECIPE

The bizcochito is a crunchy little cookie that has been a favorite treat in New Mexico for years. In fact, it's so popular that it was adopted as the official state cookie.

BIZCOCHITOS

1 cup lard or butter
¾ cup sugar
1 egg, beaten
½ tablespoon baking powder

½ teaspoon salt
½ tablespoon anise seed
2 cups all-purpose flour
¼ cup orange juice

Topping:

1 tablespoon ground cinnamon

1 tablespoon sugar

1. In a large bowl, combine the lard or butter with the sugar and egg. Mix until smooth.
2. In a medium bowl, combine the baking powder, salt, anise seed, and ½ cup of the flour. Add this mixture to the first bowl and mix well.
3. Gradually stir in the orange juice.
4. Stir in the remaining 1½ cups of flour until the mixture is a stiff dough. On a countertop or board that has been dusted with flour, knead the dough with your hands.
5. Return the dough to the large bowl and cover it with a kitchen towel. Refrigerate the dough until it is chilled.
6. In a small bowl, mix together the cinnamon and sugar for the topping.
7. Ask an adult to help you preheat the oven to 350° F.
8. Remove the dough from the refrigerator and use a rolling pin to roll it out until it is about ¼ inch thick. Use cookie cutters or the rim of a glass to cut out cookies.
9. Sprinkle cookies with cinnamon-and-sugar mixture and place them on a cookie sheet.
10. Bake for 10 to 12 minutes, or until cookies are golden brown. Makes about 4 dozen.

HISTORICAL TIMELINE

10,000 B.C. People first begin to arrive in what later became New Mexico.

A.D. 1276 A 23-year-long drought begins.

1540 Francisco Vásquez de Coronado begins searching for the Seven Cities of Cibola.

1610 Pedro de Peralta founds Santa Fe.

1680 The Pueblo Revolt takes place.

1693 Spain reconquers New Mexico and many Pueblo Indians leave the colony.

1740 The Comanche Indians control parts of New Mexico.

1786 New Mexican and Comanche leaders sign a peace treaty.

1821 Mexico wins its independence from Spain; the Santa Fe Trail opens.

1846 General Stephen Kearny claims New Mexico for the United States; the Mexican War (1846–1848) begins.

1850 The U.S. government establishes the Territory of New Mexico.

1863 Many Indians die during the Long Walk to the Bosque Redondo Reservation.

1878 Railroad tracks are laid across New Mexico.

1881 William H. Bonney, also known as Billy the Kid, is killed by Sherrif Pat Garrett near Fort Sumner. A notorious outlaw, Bonney murdered 21 people.

1912 New Mexico becomes the 47th state.

1945 The world's first atomic bomb is tested near Alamogordo.

1979 The U.S. Congress approves of building the Waste Isolation Pilot Plant near Carlsbad.

1982 The Space Shuttle *Columbia* lands at White Sands Space Harbor near Alamogordo.

1999 The WIPP facility begins receiving shipments of low-level nuclear waste.

2000 A wildfire burns thousands of acres of land in north central New Mexico.

2001 The Very Large Array (VLA) radio telescope in Socorro celebrates its 20th anniversary.

OUTSTANDING NEW MEXICANS

Mary Austin

William H. Bonney

Bruce Cabot

Rudolfo Anaya (born 1937) was born in the small village of Pastura, New Mexico. Many of his books, including *Bless Me, Ultima* and *Rio Grande Fall*, are about New Mexico's Latino heritage, people, and legends. Anaya also writes books for children.

Mary Austin (1868–1934) was a writer who settled in Santa Fe in 1924. Her house became a meeting place for many important writers in the area. Austin's books, which describe the lives of Indians in the Southwest, include *The Land of Little Rain* and *Isidro*.

William H. Bonney (1859?–1881), better known as Billy the Kid, moved from New York to Silver City, New Mexico, in 1868. He soon became feared as a cattle thief and gunfighter. Bonney managed to escape from jail several times.

Bruce Cabot (1904–1972), an actor, played the hero who saved actress Fay Wray from the oversized gorilla in the 1933 film *King Kong*. Cabot was born in Carlsbad, New Mexico.

John Denver (1943–1997) was a singer and songwriter. "Take Me Home, Country Roads" and "Rocky Mountain High" are two of his well-known country songs. Denver was born in Roswell, New Mexico.

Chee Dodge (1860–1947), from Crystal, New Mexico, founded and chaired the Navajo Tribal Council, the first official government of the Navajo Indians. He led the council from 1923 through the 1930s, helping the tribe work with the U.S. government.

John Denver

Florence Hawley Ellis (1917–1991) taught anthropology, or the study of human culture, at the University of New Mexico. Ellis also led important archaeological digs at sites near Santa Fe and in the Chaco Canyon.

William Hanna

William Hanna (1910–2001), with his partner Joseph Barbera, created many popular cartoons for television. *The Yogi Bear Show*, *Tom and Jerry*, *The Jetsons*, and *The Flintstones* are just a few of the cartoons that Hanna-Barbera Productions has made. Hanna was born in Melrose, New Mexico.

Conrad Hilton

Conrad Hilton (1887–1979) formed the Hilton Hotel Corporation in 1946. The company runs hotels and restaurants throughout the world. Hilton was born in San Antonio, New Mexico.

Ralph Kiner (born 1922), of Santa Rita, New Mexico, played baseball from 1946 to 1955, mainly with the Pittsburgh Pirates. For seven straight seasons, Kiner hit more home runs than any other player in the National League. Kiner later became a sportscaster.

Nancy Lopez

Nancy Lopez (born 1957) is a championship golfer. She grew up in Roswell and won her first tournament when she was nine years old. Lopez is a member of the Ladies Professional Golf Association Tour Hall of Fame and the Professional Golfers' Association World Hall of Fame.

Maria Montoya Martínez (1887–1980) encouraged Native American artists to practice the arts of their ancestors. Martínez, a Pueblo Indian, was a potter from San Ildefonso Pueblo, New Mexico. She was known for her black-on-black pottery.

Maria Montoya Martínez

Bill Mauldin

Bill Mauldin (born 1921) won the Pulitzer Prize in 1945 and again in 1959 for his cartoons of U.S. Army GIs, or soldiers, Willie and Joe. His characters first appeared during World War II in *Stars and Stripes*, the U.S. Army newspaper, and later became popular throughout the country. Mauldin is from Mountain Park, New Mexico.

Amanda McKerrow (born 1964) is a ballerina from Albuquerque. In 1981 she won the gold medal at the Moscow International Ballet Competition. McKerrow is a principal dancer with the American Ballet Theatre.

Mark Medoff

Mark Medoff (born 1940) is a playwright and a professor of drama at New Mexico State University. One of Medoff's plays, *Children of a Lesser God*, was performed on Broadway before being made into an award-winning motion picture in 1986. He has also co-written an opera, *Sara McKinnon*, which is set in the Southwest and was performed at New Mexico State University in 2001.

Joseph Montoya

Joseph Montoya (1915–1978) was elected to the New Mexico House of Representatives when he was only 21 years old. In 1965 he became the first Latino politician to be elected to the U.S. Senate. Montoya was born in Peña Blanca, New Mexico.

Demi Moore (born 1962) is an actress from Roswell, New Mexico. Moore began her television career on the daytime soap opera *General Hospital*. She has since starred in several movies, including *Ghost*, *A Few Good Men*, and *G.I. Jane*.

Demi Moore

John Nichols (born 1940) has written several novels. While living in Taos, Nichols wrote a set of stories that take place in northern New Mexico—*The Milagro Beanfield War*, *The Magic Journey*, and *The Nirvana Blues*.

Georgia O'Keeffe

Georgia O'Keeffe (1887–1986), a painter, spent a lot of time visiting New Mexico before finally moving to a house near Abiquiu in 1950. Many of her paintings feature the wildflowers, sand dunes, and animal skulls of the state's deserts.

Popé (1630?–1692), from San Juan Pueblo, was an American Indian religious leader who led the Pueblo Indians in driving the Spaniards out of New Mexico in 1680. After the Spaniards returned to the territory, they allowed more religious freedom throughout the Pueblo communities.

Harrison Schmitt

Harrison Schmitt (born 1935), of Santa Rita, New Mexico, piloted the *Apollo 17* lunar module—a spacecraft used for traveling to the moon—in 1972. From 1977 to 1983, the former astronaut served as a U.S. senator from New Mexico.

Al Unser (born 1939) and **Bobby Unser** (born 1934) are two of the country's most famous race-car drivers. The brothers were born and raised in Albuquerque in a large family of racers and have won seven Indianapolis 500 races. Al's son, Al Unser Jr., is also a racer and has won the Indy 500 twice.

Bobby Unser

Pablita Velarde (born 1918), a painter from Santa Clara Pueblo, New Mexico, is one of the most famous Native American painters in the world. In her work, she applies painting techniques and styles from Tewa Indian heritage.

Pablita Velarde

FACTS-AT-A-GLANCE

Nickname: Land of Enchantment

Songs: "O, Fair New Mexico, " "Asi es Nuevo Méjico"

Motto: *Crescit Eundo* (It Grows as It Goes)

Flower: yucca flower

Tree: piñon

Bird: roadrunner

Insect: tarantula hawk wasp

Fossil: Coelophysis (dinosaur)

Gemstone: turquoise

Vegetables: chili pepper and pinto bean

Date and ranking of statehood:
January 6, 1912, the 47th state

Capital: Santa Fe

Area: 121,364 square miles

Rank in area, nationwide: 5th

Average January temperature: 34° F

Average July temperature: 74° F

New Mexico's flag combines the state's Spanish and Native American heritages. The colors of the flag are yellow and red, similar to the colors of the Spanish flag, and the design in the center of the state flag is a sun symbol used by the Zia band of the Pueblo Indians.

POPULATION GROWTH

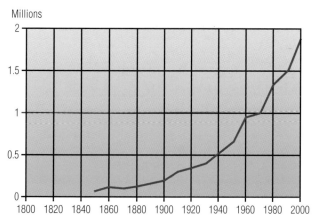

Millions

This chart shows how New Mexico's population has grown from 1850 to 2000.

The state seal of New Mexico shows a bald eagle holding its wing over a smaller Mexican eagle. This image symbolizes the transition of New Mexico from a Mexican territory to a U.S. state.

Population: 1,819,046 (2000 census)

Rank in population, nationwide: 36th

Major cities and populations: (2000 census) Albuquerque (448,607), Las Cruces (74,267), Santa Fe (62,203), Rio Rancho (51,765), Roswell (45,293)

U.S. senators: 2

U.S. representatives: 3

Electoral votes: 5

Natural resources: coal, copper, forests, gold, molybdenum, natural gas, oil, potash, silver, uranium

Agricultural products: apples, beef cattle, chili peppers, corn, cotton, dairy cattle, hay, pecans, sheep, wheat

Manufactured goods: appliances, communications equipment, computer parts, electrical equipment, food products, nuclear products, petroleum products, wood products

WHERE NEW MEXICANS WORK

Services—62 percent (services includes jobs in trade; community, social, and personal services; finance, insurance, and real estate; transportation, communication, and utilities)

Government—20 percent

Manufacturing—6 percent

Construction—6 percent

Agriculture—4 percent

Mining—2 percent

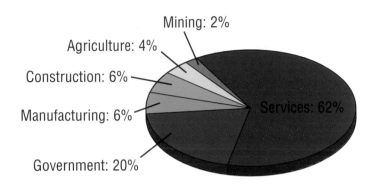

GROSS STATE PRODUCT

Services—52 percent

Manufacturing—17 percent

Government—17 percent

Mining—7 percent

Construction—5 percent

Agriculture—2 percent

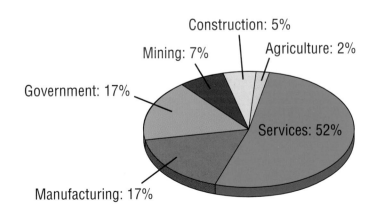

NEW MEXICO WILDLIFE

Mammals: bighorn sheep, black bear, bobcat, coyote, elk, fox, jackrabbit, javelina, kangaroo rat, marmot, mountain lion, mule deer, otter, pika, prairie dog, pronghorn antelope

Birds: duck, American kestrel, burrowing owl, golden eagle, grouse, meadowlark, pheasant, quail, red-tailed hawk, road-runner, sandhill crane, sandpiper, snow goose, wild turkey

Amphibians and reptiles: barking frog, collared lizard, coral snake, Great Plains skink, New Mexico milk snake, rattlesnake, tiger salamander, Texas horned toad, western painted turtle, yellow mud turtle

Fish: bluegill, catfish, cutthroat trout, largemouth bass, rainbow trout, sunfish, black bass

Trees: aspen, cottonwood, Douglas-fir, Gambel oak, juniper, piñon, ponderosa pine, white fir, willow

Wild plants: alpine fungi, blue columbine, cholla cactus, desert anemone, mesquite, prickly pear, purple prairie clover, sagebrush, yucca

Central New Mexico's Bosque del Apache National Wildlife Refuge is a winter home for sandhill cranes.

PLACES TO VISIT

Bradbury Science Museum, Los Alamos

Visitors to this museum, which is part of the Los Alamos National Laboratory, learn about the history of the atom bomb, nuclear research, lasers, and more. Demonstrations, videos, and hands-on exhibits provide an interactive experience.

Carlsbad Caverns National Park, near Carlsbad

This national park boasts one of the largest underground cave systems in the world, and the many caverns are filled with amazing stalactites, stalagmites, and other natural formations. During the summer, the caverns are home to a large colony of bats, and brave visitors can stay until dusk to watch as thousands of bats leave the caves to feed.

Chaco Culture National Historical Park, near Nageezi

The ruins of Anasazi Indian communities are scattered throughout this national park, including the large Pueblo Bonito, which once had more than five hundred rooms. The visitor's center and museum offer information on the history of the Anasazi and their dwellings.

Museum of New Mexico, Santa Fe

The Museum of New Mexico is actually made up of four Santa Fe museums. Visitors can purchase one pass for admission to the Museum of Fine Arts, the Museum of Indian Arts and Culture, the Museum of International Folk Art, and the Palace of the Governors (a museum of New Mexican history).

Petroglyph National Monument, Albuquerque

Thousands of petroglyphs (designs carved in stone) of people, animals, and symbols cover the dark rocks of the Petroglyph National Monument. Historians believe that these carvings were done by Native Americans and possibly Spanish settlers, and that some of them are more than 700 years old.

San Miguel Mission, Santa Fe

Built in the early 1600s by the Indian servants of Spanish missionaries, this small adobe building is the oldest church still in use in the United States. Paintings, artifacts, and a bell that may date back to the 1300s are some of the sights inside.

Taos Pueblo, just north of Taos

Pueblo Indians have inhabited the Taos Pueblo for hundreds of years. Respectful visitors are welcome to tour this World Heritage Site, where they can stroll around the central plaza, sample local taste treats, shop for handicrafts and art, and even attend special ceremonies.

White Sands National Monument, near Alamogordo

Take a hike through the White Sands National Monument to see a unique landscape of white-gypsum sand dunes. Sharp-eyed visitors might catch a glimpse of area wildlife, much of which has developed light coloring to survive here, and during the summer the park stays open late for full moons, which light up the sand for miles.

San Miguel Mission in Santa Fe

ANNUAL EVENTS

Kings' Day celebrations, at most Indian pueblos—*January*

Frontier Days, Fort Selden State Monument near Las Cruces—*April*

Cinco de Mayo celebrations, statewide—*May*

Smokey Bear Stampede, Capitan—*July*

UFO Festival, Roswell—*July*

Inter-Tribal Indian Ceremonial, Gallup—*August*

Great American Duck Race, Deming—*August*

New Mexico State Fair, Albuquerque—*September*

International Balloon Fiesta, Albuquerque—*October*

Northern Navajo Nation Fair, Shiprock—*October*

Festival of the Cranes, Bosque del Apache National Wildlife Refuge, near Socorro—*November*

Winter Spanish Market, Santa Fe—*December*

LEARN MORE ABOUT NEW MEXICO

BOOKS

General

Fradin, Judith Bloom, and Dennis Brindell Fradin. *New Mexico.* Chicago: Children's Press, 1993.

McDaniel, Melissa. *New Mexico.* New York: Benchmark Books, 1999. For older readers.

Special Interest

Freedman, Russell. *In the Days of the Vaqueros: America's First True Cowboys.* Boston: Clarion Books, 2001. This book explores the lives of the original cowboys of the Wild West, and describes the origins of many cowboy traditions.

La Pierre, Yvette. *Welcome to Josefina's World, 1824: Growing Up on America's Southwest Frontier.* Middleton, WI: Pleasant Company Publications, 1999. This nonfiction book examines daily life in New Mexico during the 1800s, from bargaining to bathing.

Lowery, Linda. *Georgia O'Keeffe.* Minneapolis, MN: Carolrhoda Books, Inc., 1996. This biography of Georgia O'Keeffe describes the artist's life, her work, and the way she fell in love with New Mexico and its landscape.

Naranjo, Tito E. *A Day with a Pueblo.* Minneapolis, MN: Runestone Press, 2000. A combination of facts and fiction illustrates modern life among the Pueblo people of Taos, New Mexico.

Velarde, Pablita. *Old Father Story Teller.* Santa Fe, NM: Clear Light Publishers, 1989. The famous Native American artist retells and illustrates some of her favorite traditional Indian legends.

Fiction

Anaya, Rudolfo. *The Farolitos of Christmas.* New York: Hyperion Books for Children, 1995. This richly illustrated book by a New Mexican writer describes the origins of farolitos, the luminarias set out at Christmastime in Latino villages and neighborhoods.

Meyer, Carolyn. *Rio Grande Stories.* San Diego, CA: Harcourt Brace, 1994. Students in an Albuquerque school are assigned the task of gathering stories about local people, heritage, and customs. Join them and see what they find. For older readers.

O'Dell, Scott. *Sing Down the Moon.* New York: Bantam Doubleday Dell Books for Young Readers, 1999. First published in 1970, this Newbery Award Honor Book is the gripping tale of a young Navajo Indian who is captured by Spanish settlers in New Mexico. For older readers.

Stevens, Jan Romero. *Carlos and the Cornfield.* Flagstaff, AZ: Northland Publishing, 1995. This story, told in English and Spanish, describes Carlos's life on a New Mexican farm and is a fun read for beginning learners of either language.

Turner, Ann. *The Girl Who Chased Away Sorrow: The Diary of Sarah Nita, a Navajo Girl.* New York: Scholastic, 1999. This fictional diary tells the story of the Long Walk (the forced migration of New Mexican Indians to Bosque Redondo Reservation) from the point of view of a young girl.

WEBSITES

¡Bienvenidos a Nuevo Mexico! (Welcome to New Mexico!)
<http://www.state.nm.us>
The official website of New Mexico offers information about living, working, and traveling in the state, as well as fun facts and more.

New Mexico Department of Tourism
<http://www.newmexico.org>
Maps, news, and upcoming events are just a few of the helpful things visitors can find at the home page of New Mexico's office of tourism.

The Albuquerque Journal Online
<http://www.abqjournal.com>
The website of the *Albuquerque Journal,* New Mexico's largest daily newspaper, provides online articles and information about the state's news, weather, and sports.

New Mexico Culturenet
<http://www.nmcn.org>
This website focuses on the rich culture and heritage of New Mexico and its people.

PRONUNCIATION GUIDE

Alamogordo (al-uh-muh-GAWRD-oh)

Albuquerque (AL-buh-kuhr-kee)

Anasazi (ahn-uh-SAHZ-ee)

Apache (uh-PACH-ee)

Comanche (kuh-MAN-chee)

Gila (HEE-luh)

Las Cruces (lahs KROO-sehs)

Los Alamos (lohs AL-uh-mohs)

Navajo (NAV-uh-hoh)

Pueblo (poo-EHB-loh)

Rio Grande (ree-oh GRAND) or (ree-oh GRAHN-day)

San Juan (san WAHN)

Santa Fe (sant-uh FAY)

Taos (TAUS)

Sparklers amuse two young New Mexicans on the Fourth of July.

GLOSSARY

Anglo: historically, a white person who lives in the United States. Mostly used in the Southwest, the term has come to include African and Asian Americans.

basin: a bowl-shaped region. Also, the land drained by a river and its branches.

colony: a territory ruled by a country some distance away

desert: an area that receives about 10 inches or less of rain or snow a year

drought: a long period of extreme dryness due to lack of rain or snow

Dust Bowl: an area of the Great Plains that suffered from long dry spells and dust storms, especially during the 1930s

irrigation: a method of watering land by directing water through canals, ditches, pipes, or sprinklers

Latino: a person living in the United States who either came from or has ancestors from Latin America (Mexico and much of Central and South America)

lava: hot, melted rock that erupts from a volcano or from cracks in the earth's surface and that hardens as it cools

mesa: an isolated hill with steep sides and a flat top

nuclear waste: waste that gives off dangerous rays of energy and particles called radiation

plateau: a large, relatively flat area that stands above the surrounding land

radiation: rays of energy and particles given off when atoms and molecules change to other elements. Radiation is often harmful to living things.

radioactive: giving off rays of energy called radiation when the atoms of certain elements change to other elements

reservation: public land set aside by the government for Native Americans

treaty: an agreement between two or more groups, usually having to do with peace or trade

INDEX

agriculture, 12, 13, 17, 19, 22, 25, 29, 31, 32, 33, 37, 49, 50. *See also* chili peppers; corn; livestock and ranching
Alamogordo, 38, 61
Albuquerque, 29, 34, 39, 40, 41, 43, 44, 45, 71
Anglos, 27, 29, 40, 42, 43
animals, 13, 16, 17, 19, 24, 25, 32, 34, 35, 37, 45, 50, 60, 71, 73; State Wildlife, 73
Arizona, 7, 28, 60
arts and crafts, 17, 23, 24, 39, 40, 42–44. *See also* pottery
atomic bomb and nuclear weapons, 38–39, 43, 48, 49, 51–59, 61

Basin and Range region, 10, 11, 12
Becknell, William, 26
Billy the Kid, 35

chili peppers, 12, 49, 50
cities and towns, 15, 20, 21, 24, 26–27, 28, 29, 33, 34, 35, 37, 38, 39, 40, 41, 42, 43, 44, 45, 46, 53, 54, 55, 57, 60, 61. *See also* Albuquerque; Los Alamos; Santa Fe; Taos
climate, 13, 15, 16, 49
Colorado, 7, 28, 60
Colorado Plateau region, 10, 11
Continental Divide, 11, 14
corn, 17, 32, 50
Coronado, Francisco Vásquez de, 20–22

deserts, 7, 12, 15, 16, 38
Dust Bowl, 36–37

economy, 24, 32, 36, 37, 40–50, 56; gross state product, 72; workforce, 72
energy sources, 38–39, 42, 49, 53. *See also* atomic bomb and nuclear weapons

environment, 51–59
ethnic makeup, 40–42

festivals and holidays, 34, 43–44, 61
fish and fishing, 15, 42, 45, 73
flag, 70
food, 22, 24, 31, 42, 48, 61; recipe, 63
forests and forestry, 7, 42, 48, 60, 73

Gadsden Purchase, 28
Garrett, Pat, 35
ghost towns, 33
gold and silver, 20, 21, 22, 33
Great Plains region, 10, 13, 16, 50

health and diseases, 22, 31, 52, 53, 56–57, 58
history, 17–39; ancient, 10, 17–18; colonization, 20–24; 1800s, 26–35; exploration and trade, 20, 21, 22, 25, 26, 27, 29, 32; 1900s, 36–39, 60, 61; settlers, 17–34; 1700s, 25–26; statehood, 36, 71; timeline, 64–65
housing, 18–19, 21

Indians, 17–26, 29, 31, 32, 37, 39, 40, 41, 42, 43, 44, 61, 70; Anasazi, 17, 18, 19, 21; Apache, 19, 24, 31, 32, 40, 41, 42, 61; reservations, 31, 32, 41, 42; Comanche, 25, 26; Mogollon, 17; Navajo, 17, 19, 24, 31, 32, 40, 41, 42, 61; Pueblos, 21, 22, 23, 24, 25, 26, 29, 40, 41, 43, 61, 70; Ute, 25, 41; Zia, 70

jobs, 33, 36, 38, 39, 40, 46, 48, 49, 56
Jornada del Muerto (Journey of Death), 24–25

Kearny, Stephen, 28

languages, 14, 17, 21, 23, 36, 37, 39, 61
Latinos, 40, 41, 42, 43, 44, 70

livestock and ranching, 13, 32, 33, 34, 35, 37, 48, 49, 50
Los Alamos, 15, 37, 38, 43, 53

manufacturing and industries, 32, 33, 34, 38, 39, 46–50
maps, 8, 9, 47; economic, 47; physical, 9; political, 8
Mexico, 7, 20, 21, 22, 24, 26, 28, 44, 71
military, 20, 23, 28, 29, 31, 35, 37
mining and minerals, 33, 34, 42, 49
mountains, 7, 10, 11, 12, 15, 16. *See also* Rocky Mountains (Rockies)
museums and historical sites, 18, 19, 43
music, dance, and theater, 43, 44

National forests and parks, 7, 12, 46, 48, 60, 73
Native Americans. *See* Indians
New Mexico: Annual Events, 76; boundaries, size, and location, 7, 10–15, 28; ethnic makeup, 40–42; Facts-at-a-Glance, 70–73; flag, 70; Fun Facts, 60–61; Historical Timeline, 64–65; maps, 8, 9, 47; nicknames, 7; origin of name, 22; Outstanding New Mexicans, 66–69; Places to Visit, 74–75; population, 40, 41, 42, 71; recipe, 63; statehood, 36, 71; State Song, 62; state symbols, 70–71; wildlife, 73
nuclear waste, 51–59

Oppenheimer, J. Robert, 37, 51

Peralta, Pedro de, 22
plants, 12, 16, 73
pollution, 53
Popé, 23
population, 40, 41, 42, 71

pottery, 17, 24, 39, 42

radiation, 51, 52, 53, 57
railroads, 34
religion, 19, 22, 23, 43
Rio Grande, 13, 14, 45
Rio Grande Valley, 12, 50
rivers and streams, 11, 13, 14, 15, 45, 50, 53. *See also* Rio Grande
Rocky Mountain region, 10, 11
Rocky Mountains, 10, 11, 16

Santa Fe, 22, 26–27, 28, 29, 37, 40, 42, 43, 45, 46, 57, 60, 71
Santa Fe Trail, 26, 27
Seven Cities of Cibola, 20, 21
Smokey Bear, 60
Spain, 14, 20–26, 29
sports and recreation, 15, 42–46

Taos, 15, 43, 44
Taos Pueblo, 21
Territory of New Mexico, 28–36
tourism, 18, 42–46
trade, 25, 26, 27, 29, 32

United States, 10, 21, 26, 27, 28, 37, 38, 44, 48, 60
U.S. government, 28, 29, 32, 37, 39, 46, 55, 56, 58, 59

Very Large Array radio telescope, 39

wars and conflicts, 23, 24, 25, 26, 28, 29, 30, 31, 32, 35, 37, 38, 51
Waste Isolation Pilot Plant (WIPP), 54–59
Wild West, 35

PHOTO ACKNOWLEDGMENTS

Cover photographs by © Karl Weatherly/CORBIS (left) and © David Muench/ CORBIS (right); PresentationMaps.com, pp. 1, 8, 9, 47; © Reinhard Eisele/Corbis, pp. 2–3; © Liz Hymans/Corbis, p. 3; © Christie's Images/CORBIS, pp. 4, 7 (inset), 17 (inset), 40 (inset), 51 (inset); © Tom Bean/CORBIS, p. 6; © Charles S. Swenson, pp. 10, 12 (top), 16 (top); © Stephen Trimble/Root Resources, p. 11; © Kent & Donna Dannen, pp. 12 (bottom), 13, 19, 21, 42 (bottom), 45, 48 (top); © James Blank/Root Resources, pp. 14, 41; © Frederica Georgia, pp. 15, 24, 42 (top), 80; © Robert E. Barber, pp. 16 (bottom), 18, 40, 73; Library of Congress, pp. 20, 28, 51; © Tony LaGruth, p. 22; The Southwest Museum, Los Angeles, Photo #CT.551, p. 23; Edward E. Ayer Collection, The Newberry Library, Chicago, p. 25; Museum of New Mexico, pp. 27 (neg. #6977), 30 (neg. #152188), 32 (Edward S. Curtis, neg. #143874), 34 (bottom, Ben Wittick, School of American Research Collections, neg. #15870), 35 (neg. #92018), 67 (bottom, Wyatt Davis, neg. #4591), 69 (top, neg. #9763), 69 (bottom, neg. #174193); New Mexico State Records Center and Archives, pp. 31 (F. McNitt Collection, neg. #5702), 34 (top, D. Woodward Collection, neg. #22697), 37 (R. V. Hunter Collection, neg. #23057); Center for Southwest Research, General Library, University of New Mexico, pp. 33 (Henry A. Schmidt, neg. #000-179-0736), 66 (top, neg. #00-255-0461); Kansas Collection, University of Kansas Libraries, p. 36; U. S. Army, p. 38; © Stan Osolinski/Root Resources, p. 39; Ron Behrmann, Albuquerque Convention & Visitors Bureau, p. 43; Ray Lutz, Taos County Chamber of Commerce, p. 44 (top); Betty Groskin, p. 44 (bottom); © Theresa Early, p. 46 (left); Mark Nohl, New Mexico Economic & Tourism Dept., pp. 46 (right), 48 (bottom); © Jack Parsons, p. 49; © D. Newman/ Visuals Unlimited, p. 50; U. S. Deptartment of Energy, pp. 52, 55, 56, 57; Jerry Miller, Northern States Power, p. 53; AP/Wide World Photos, pp. 58, 67 (second from bottom); © Michel Monteaux, p. 59; © Harold Walter, p. 60; Toby Schnobrich, p. 61; Tim Seeley, pp. 63, 71 (top), 72; Independent Picture Service, pp. 66 (second from top), 68 (second from bottom); RCA, p. 66 (bottom); Photofest, pp. 66 (second from bottom), 68 (bottom); Cleveland Public Library Photograph Collection, p. 67 (top); Hilton Hotels Corporation, p. 67 (second from top); © Archive Photos, p. 68 (top); New Mexico State University, p. 68 (second from top); NASA, p. 69 (second from top); Indianapolis Motor Speedway, p. 69 (second from bottom); Jean Matheny, p. 70 (top) © Phil Schermeister/CORBIS, p. 75.